# BEARS

# Grizzly Bears

## Stuart A. Kallen

ABDO & Daughters

**visit us at
www.abdopub.com**

Published by Abdo & Daughters, 4940 Viking Drive, Suite 622, Edina, Minnesota 55435.

Copyright © 1998 by Abdo Consulting Group, Inc., Pentagon Tower, P.O. Box 36036, Minneapolis, Minnesota 55435 USA. International copyrights reserved in all countries. No part of this book may be reproduced in any form without written permission from the publisher.

Printed in the United States.

Cover Photo credits: Peter Arnold, Inc.
Interior Photo credits: Peter Arnold, Inc.

Edited by Lori Kinstad Pupeza

## Library of Congress Cataloging-in-Publication Data

Kallen, Stuart A., 1955-
     Grizzly bears / Stuart A. Kallen
     p.   cm. -- (Bears)
     Includes index.
     Summary: Describes the physical characteristics, habitat, and behavior of this subspecies of brown bear.
     ISBN 1-56239-591-2
     1. Grizzly bear--Juvenile literature. [1. Grizzly bear. 2. Bears.] I. Title. II. Series: Kallen, Stuart A., 1955-   Bears.
     QL737.C27K344   1998
     599.74'446--dc20
                                     96-707
                                     CIP
                                     AC

# Contents

# Grizzly Bears and Their Family

Grizzly bears are **mammals**. Like humans, they breathe air with lungs, are **warm blooded**, and nurse their young with milk.

Bears first **evolved** around 40 million years ago. They were small, meat-eating, tree-climbing animals. The early bears were related to coyotes, wolves, foxes, raccoons, and even dogs. Today, there are eight different **species** of bear. They live in 50 countries on 3 **continents**.

The grizzly bear is a member of the brown bear family. There are about 10 **subspecies** of brown bear. The grizzly bear is one of them. Other subspecies of brown bear are the huge Alaskan brown bear and the giant Kodiak brown bear.

The scientific name for the grizzly bear is *Ursus arctos horribilis.* That means "horrible bear" in Latin.

**A family of grizzly bears.**

# Size, Shape, and Color

Grizzly bears are medium-sized bears. Grizzly bears are about 7 to 10 feet (2.1 to 3.1 m) when standing up on their hind legs.

Grizzlies may weigh from 350 to 700 pounds (158 to 317 kg). Males are about 40 percent larger than females. The largest grizzly ever recorded weighed 1,500 pounds (679 kg).

The name "grizzly" is a term used to describe the animal's coloring. It has a dark coat with shimmering silver-tipped hairs that give it a "grizzled" look.

The grizzly is strongly built with a hump of fat and muscle over the shoulder. Grizzlies have thick heads with "dished-in" faces. Their ears are short and round.

Their eyes are small for so large an animal. Grizzly bears have large, pointed teeth that help them catch and kill **prey**. They can stand up easily on their large, wide feet. Each toe ends in a long, curving claw.

*A grizzly bear in a meadow.*

# Where They Live

Grizzly bears roam far and wide. They live in the United States in Alaska, Idaho, Montana, Washington, and Wyoming. Grizzlies live in the Canadian **provinces** of Alberta, British Columbia, the Northwest Territories, and the Yukon. Grizzlies have even been spotted in the Mexican state of Chihuahua, but are now extinct there.

There are about 40,000 grizzly bears living in Alaska. Their numbers are about 1,000 in Montana, 300 in Wyoming, and less than 50 in Washington and Idaho. Canada has about 25,000 grizzly bears.

Alaska

Canada

United States

*Opposite page: A grizzly sitting upright.*

8

# Senses

Bears are very smart animals that learn quickly. They are curious and have very good memories.

Because of their small eyes, there is a myth that bears cannot see well. But bears have good eyesight. They can tell the difference between colors and see well at night. They can spot moving objects at a far distance. Bears stand on their hind legs to be able to see farther.

Bears see and hear well, but their sense of smell is their most important sense. Their keen sense of smell allows them to find mates, avoid humans, locate their **cubs**, and gather food. Bears have been known to detect a human scent 14 hours after a person has passed along a trail. Experiments have proven that bears can smell food three miles away!

*Grizzly bears often stand up to see farther.*

# Defense

Grizzly bears have long been feared by humans. Although shy and peaceful most of the time, they can be deadly when bothered.

Grizzly bears are very strong. They move rocks and large logs with one paw. A grizzly bear may kill a moose, elk, or deer with a single blow to the neck. Grizzly bears have 20 long claws and can easily rip the bark off trees. Scientists have seen grizzlies bite clear through pine trees 8 inches (20 cm) thick.

When hunting large game, bears may stalk it like a cat. There is a myth that bears are slow. But they are surprisingly quick. A grizzly can easily run 35 to 40 mph (56-64 kmph) for short distances.

Most bears would rather run away from a human than attack. Bears attack when protecting their young, if their escape routes are blocked, if they are protecting food sources, or if they are startled.

*Grizzly bears have very large teeth.*

# Food

Grizzly bears eat just about anything. To fuel such huge bodies, they must eat huge amounts of food every day. Bears need fat to get them through the long, cold winter.

Grizzlies will eat plants but eagerly seek out animals for food. The bears will fish for salmon or trout. A bear may eat up to twelve or more large fish in one afternoon.

Grizzlies will also eat food that has been washed up on the sand by the ocean. This may be seaweed, crabs, or dead fish. Away from the water, brown bears will eat moose, deer, elk, and caribou.

When grizzly bears see humans, they think of only one thing—food. Cabins, camps, garbage cans, and town dumps are often raided by bears looking for easy meals. Once bears get a taste for human food, they are hard to stop. Never, ever feed a bear.

A grizzly bear feeding on berries.

# Bear Hibernation

As summer ends, grizzly bears become very fat. They also drink huge amounts of water.

As winter comes, the bears find a cave or hollow log to move into. This is called a **den.** The bear must be safe inside its den all winter long.

By September or October the bears are fast asleep—**hibernating**—in their dens. By the time winter comes, the bear is in a deep sleep.

When spring comes, the bears wake up. They yawn, stretch, and limp out of the den, weighing half as much as they did in the fall. Female bears will have **cubs** that were born at the end of the hibernation. The bears are hungry and need to drink large amounts of water. Soon they are hunting for food again.

The bears continue to lose weight for a few months until summer comes and food is once again plentiful.

*A grizzly bear coming out of its den in early spring.*

# Babies

Females can first start to have babies when they are about five years old.

Bears usually mate in June and July. Female bears are pregnant for about eight months. **Cubs** are born in January or February while the mother is sleeping in the **den**.

The cubs are very tiny, and weigh between 8.5 and 11.5 ounces (240 to 330 g). They are blind, bald, and helpless. By the time they are five weeks old, they learn to walk. By springtime, cubs are ready to leave the den. The first spring outside the den is tough for baby grizzly bears. Cubs may be killed by eagles, bobcats, or mountain lions.

By the time they are 6 months old, bear cubs weigh 55 to 65 pounds (25 to 30 kg). The cubs will spend two winters in the den with their mother.

After that, the mother will force them to go out on their own.

*A grizzly cub holding onto a tree trunk.*

# Grizzly Bear Facts

**Scientific Name:** *Ursus arctos horribilus*

**Average Size:** Grizzly bears are medium-sized bears. The average adult is 35 inches (89 cm) high when standing on all 4 feet. Grizzly bears are about 7 to 10 feet (2.1 to 3.1 m) tall when standing up on their hind legs.

Grizzlies may weigh from 350 to 700 pounds (158 to 317 kg). Males are about 40 percent larger than females. The largest grizzly ever recorded weighed 1,500 pounds (679 kg).

**Where They're Found:** Grizzly bears live in the United States in Alaska, Idaho, Montana, Washington, and Wyoming. Grizzlies live in the Canadian **provinces** of Alberta, British Columbia, the Northwest Territories, and the Yukon.

*A grizzly bear in Alaska.*

# Glossary

**continent** (KAHN-tih-nent) - one of the seven main land masses: Europe, Asia, Africa, North America, South America, Australia, and Antarctica. Grizzly bears are found only in North America.

**cub** - a baby bear.

**den** - a cave, hole in the ground, or hole in a tree used by a bear for a shelter.

**evolve** - for a species to develop or change over millions of years.

**hibernate** - to spend the winter in a deep sleep.

**mammal** - a class of animals, including humans, that have hair and feed their young milk.

**nurse** - to feed a young animal or child milk from the mother's breast.

**prey** - an animal hunted and captured for food.

**province** - a division of a country like a state. Canada is divided into 12 provinces.

**species** (SPEE-sees) - a group of related living things that have the same basic characteristics.

**subspecies** (sub SPEE-sees) - a group of related living things that has minor physical differences from the main species it belongs to.

**warm blooded** - an animal whose body temperature remains the same and warmer than the outside air or temperature.

# Index